# Saudi Arabia
# in the New Middle East

**COUNCIL** *on*
**FOREIGN**
**RELATIONS**

*Center for Preventive Action*

Council Special Report No. 63
December 2011

F. Gregory Gause III

# Saudi Arabia in the New Middle East

The Council on Foreign Relations (CFR) is an independent, nonpartisan membership organization, think tank, and publisher dedicated to being a resource for its members, government officials, business executives, journalists, educators and students, civic and religious leaders, and other interested citizens in order to help them better understand the world and the foreign policy choices facing the United States and other countries. Founded in 1921, CFR carries out its mission by maintaining a diverse membership, with special programs to promote interest and develop expertise in the next generation of foreign policy leaders; convening meetings at its headquarters in New York and in Washington, DC, and other cities where senior government officials, members of Congress, global leaders, and prominent thinkers come together with CFR members to discuss and debate major international issues; supporting a Studies Program that fosters independent research, enabling CFR scholars to produce articles, reports, and books and hold roundtables that analyze foreign policy issues and make concrete policy recommendations; publishing *Foreign Affairs*, the preeminent journal on international affairs and U.S. foreign policy; sponsoring Independent Task Forces that produce reports with both findings and policy prescriptions on the most important foreign policy topics; and providing up-to-date information and analysis about world events and American foreign policy on its website, CFR.org.

The Council on Foreign Relations takes no institutional positions on policy issues and has no affiliation with the U.S. government. All views expressed in its publications and on its website are the sole responsibility of the author or authors.

Council Special Reports (CSRs) are concise policy briefs, produced to provide a rapid response to a developing crisis or contribute to the public's understanding of current policy dilemmas. CSRs are written by individual authors—who may be CFR fellows or acknowledged experts from outside the institution—in consultation with an advisory committee, and are intended to take sixty days from inception to publication. The committee serves as a sounding board and provides feedback on a draft report. It usually meets twice—once before a draft is written and once again when there is a draft for review; however, advisory committee members, unlike Task Force members, are not asked to sign off on the report or to otherwise endorse it. Once published, CSRs are posted on www.cfr.org.

For further information about CFR or this Special Report, please write to the Council on Foreign Relations, 58 East 68th Street, New York, NY 10065, or call the Communications office at 212.434.9888. Visit our website, CFR.org.

To submit a letter in response to a Council Special Report for publication on our website, CFR.org, you may send an email to CSReditor@cfr.org. Alternatively, letters may be mailed to us at: Publications Department, Council on Foreign Relations, 58 East 68th Street, New York, NY 10065. Letters should include the writer's name, postal address, and daytime phone number. Letters may be edited for length and clarity, and may be published online. Please do not send attachments. All letters become the property of the Council on Foreign Relations and will not be returned. We regret that, owing to the volume of correspondence, we cannot respond to every letter.

This report is printed on paper that is FSC® certified by Rainforest Alliance, which promotes environmentally responsible, socially beneficial, and economically viable management of the world's forests.

# Contents

# Foreword

The United States' relationship with Saudi Arabia has been one of the cornerstones of U.S. policy in the Middle East for decades. Despite their substantial differences in history, culture, and governance, the two countries have generally agreed on important political and economic issues and have often relied on each other to secure mutual aims. The 1990–91 Gulf War is perhaps the most obvious example, but their ongoing cooperation on maintaining regional stability, moderating the global oil market, and pursuing terrorists should not be downplayed.

Yet for all the relationship's importance, it is increasingly imperiled by mistrust and misunderstanding. One major question is Saudi Arabia's stability. In this Council Special Report, sponsored by the Center for Preventive Action, F. Gregory Gause III first explores the foundations of Riyadh's present stability and potential sources of future unrest. It is difficult not to notice that Saudi Arabia avoided significant upheaval during the political uprisings that swept the Middle East in 2011, despite sharing many of the social and economic problems of Egypt, Yemen, and Libya. But unlike their counterparts in Cairo, Sanaa, and Tripoli, Riyadh's leadership was able to maintain order in large part by increasing public spending on housing and salaries, relying on loyal and well-equipped security forces, and utilizing its extensive patronage networks. The divisions within the political opposition also helped the government's cause.

This is not to say that Gause believes that the stability of the House of Saud is assured. He points out that the top heirs to the throne are elderly and the potential for disorderly squabbling may increase as a new generation enters the line of succession. Moreover, the population is growing quickly, and there is little reason to believe that oil will forever be able to buy social tranquility. Perhaps most important, Gause argues, the leadership's response to the 2011 uprisings did little to forestall future crises; an opportunity for manageable political reform was mostly lost.

Turning to the regional situation, Gause finds it no less complex. Saudi Arabia has wielded considerable influence with its neighbors through its vast oil reserves, its quiet financial and political support for allies, and the ideological influence of *salafism*, the austere interpretation of Islam that is perhaps Riyadh's most controversial export. For all its wealth and religious influence, however, Saudi Arabia's recent record has been less than successful. It was unable to counter Iranian influence in post-Saddam Iraq, it could not prevent Hezbollah taking power in Lebanon, and its ongoing efforts to reconcile Hamas and the Palestinian Authority have come to naught.

The U.S.-Saudi relationship has, unsurprisingly, been affected by these and other challenges, including Saudi unhappiness with Washington's decision to distance itself from Egyptian president Hosni Mubarak, the lack of progress on the Israeli-Palestinian peace process, and Iran. For its part, the United States is unhappy with the Saudi intervention in Bahrain and Saudi support for radical Islamists around the region and the world. The two traditional anchors of the U.S.-Saudi relationship—the Cold War and U.S. operation of Riyadh's oil fields—are, Gause notes, no longer factors. It is no wonder, he contends, that the relationship is strained when problems are myriad and the old foundations of the informal alliance are gone.

It would be far better, Gause argues, to acknowledge that the two countries can no longer expect to act in close concert under such conditions. He recommends that the U.S. reimagine the relationship as simply transactional, based on cooperation when interests—rather than habit—dictate. Prioritizing those interests will therefore be critical. Rather than pressuring Riyadh for domestic political reform, or asking it to reduce global oil prices, Gause recommends that the United States spend its political capital where it really matters: on maintaining regional security, dismantling terrorist networks, and preventing the proliferation of nuclear weapons.

There have been few relationships more important to the United States than that with Saudi Arabia, and it is vital that, as it enters a new phase, the expectations and priorities of both countries are clear. In *Saudi Arabia in the New Middle East*, Gause effectively assesses the challenges and opportunities facing Saudi Arabia and makes a compelling argument for a more modest, businesslike relationship between Washington and Riyadh that better reflects modern realities. As the United States begins reassessing its commitments in the Greater Middle East, this report offers a clear vision for a more limited—but perhaps more appropriate and sustainable—future partnership.

**Richard N. Haass**
*President*
Council on Foreign Relations
December 2011

# Acknowledgments

It is a pleasure to thank those individuals and institutions that helped bring this report to fruition. CFR is the most important public policy organization dealing with foreign policy in the country, and it is an honor to publish something with it. CFR President Richard N. Haass and Director of Studies James M. Lindsay provided support and feedback on the project from the beginning. I am very grateful to them. Paul B. Stares, director of CFR's Center for Preventive Action, invited me to consider this project and was its patron and guide from conception to publication. I owe him the largest debt here. His very competent staff made things run smoothly from beginning to end, and I thank them, particularly Research Associate Andrew Miller and Assistant Director Sophia Yang, for their work. As always, CFR's expert Publications staff has turned out a very attractive product. It is nice to work with real professionals.

I am indebted to the members of the report's advisory committee for spending their valuable time reading my prose and making very useful suggestions in the two group meetings we held. They are an extremely distinguished group. The fact that they would take the time to participate in this exercise is humbling to me and evidence of CFR's unparalleled convening power. Special thanks go to the chair of the committee, Ambassador Chas Freeman, for his advice and guidance at every step of the process. I also want to acknowledge Ray Close, who read the entire report, offering feedback and support. Of course, the contents of the report and the policy recommendations I put forward are mine alone and should not be attributed to the members of the advisory committee either individually or as a group. I am particularly grateful for their participation and reactions as I know that many of them do not share my conclusions.

I was fortunate enough to spend January through April of 2010 in Saudi Arabia as a visiting fellow at the King Faisal Center for Islamic

Studies and Research in Riyadh. I thank the center for its hospitality. I also thank the many Saudis and expatriate residents of the country who opened up their offices and homes to me, helping me to try to understand the country's politics.

This publication was made possible by a grant from the Carnegie Corporation of New York. The statements made and views expressed herein are solely my own.

F. Gregory Gause III

# Map

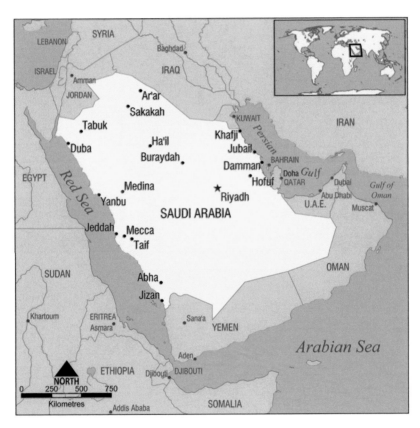

*Source:* Norman Einstein, Wikimedia Commons.

*Council Special Report*

# Introduction

There is arguably no more unlikely U.S. ally than Saudi Arabia: monarchical, deeply conservative socially, promoter of an austere and intolerant version of Islam, birthplace of Osama bin Laden and fifteen of the nineteen 9/11 hijackers. Consequently, there is no U.S. ally less well understood. Many U.S. policymakers assume that the Saudi regime is fragile, despite its remarkable record of domestic stability in the turbulent Middle East. "It is an unstable country in an unstable region," one congressional staffer said in July 2011.[1] Yet it is the Arab country least affected in its domestic politics by the Arab upheavals of 2011. Many who think it is unstable domestically also paradoxically attribute enormous power to it, to the extent that they depict it as leading a "counterrevolution" against those upheavals throughout the region.[2] One wonders just how "counterrevolutionary" the Saudis are when they have supported the NATO campaign against Muammar al-Qaddafi, successfully negotiated the transfer of power from Ali Abdullah Saleh in Yemen, and condemned the crackdown on protestors by Syrian president Bashar al-Assad, and how powerful they are when they could do little to help their ally Hosni Mubarak in Egypt.

These twin misperceptions of a country on the verge of domestic regime change yet able to exercise considerable power both in the Middle East and beyond are not new. Western observers and diplomats have been forecasting the collapse of the Saudi regime for more than sixty years. The death of the founding king, Abd al-Aziz Ibn Saud, in 1953 was supposed to lead to the unraveling of the realm.[3] The Arab nationalist challenge of Gamal Abdul Nasser in the late 1950s and early 1960s was then going to sweep it away.[4] The fall of the shah of Iran in 1979 led to a spate of speculation that monarchy's days were numbered in Arabia as well. So those questioning the regime's staying power these days are in good company.[5] The portrayal of the Saudis as leading a counterrevolutionary movement able to snuff out the Arab Spring likewise inherits a viewpoint that made Riyadh the center of regional, if not global, power in the aftermath of the 1973 oil embargo and the "kernel of evil" for its promotion of political Islam in the wake of the 9/11 attacks.[6]

The Saudis are neither fragile nor all-powerful. An effective U.S. policy toward Saudi Arabia should abandon such oversimplifications and confront the realities of both the Saudi Arabian domestic political system and Saudi regional foreign policy. Although not in crisis, as some have suggested, the relationship is no longer moored to the two anchors that stabilized it in the past: a common Cold War perspective and U.S. operation of the Saudi oil industry. Given the growing number of issues over which Washington and Riyadh have differing perspectives, it is time to recognize that the relationship is now more transactional than automatically cooperative.

In this new atmosphere, Washington needs to be clear about its priorities if it wants to get anything done with Riyadh. The United States should cooperate on issues where common interests are clear, such as stabilizing Yemen, containing Iran's regional power, and destroying al-Qaeda and its regional affiliates. It should encourage the Saudis to reconsider policies such as isolating the Iraqi government and stoking Sunni-Shia sectarian animosities that could harm both U.S. and Saudi interests in the future by making clear that overall cooperation on security issues requires these steps. Finally, U.S. policymakers should make clear that nuclear proliferation by Saudi Arabia would put at risk any future collaboration on security issues.

# Regime Stability in Saudi Arabia

Saudi Arabia has been the least affected of the major Arab states by the upheavals of 2011 that have brought down three leaders and continue to threaten others in the region. This is not because the country is uniquely immune to the social, economic, and political forces that led to regime crises elsewhere in the Arab world. Indeed, Saudi rule is as autocratic as that of Egypt under Mubarak—perhaps more so. The events of 2011 were closely followed by Saudis and inspired some demonstrations, particularly in Shia-majority areas of the Eastern Province. The demands for political reform heard throughout the Arab world were echoed in Saudi Arabia. Two important petitions that emerged during the winter of 2011 called for an elected legislature to bring the Saudi public into the decision-making process, indicating that at least some Saudis felt the same impulses that animated protestors in other Arab states.[7] Unlike the monarchs in Morocco and Jordan, however, the al-Saud regime did not even promise political reform down the line. Although Saudi Arabia is not as poor as Egypt, its per capita income is less than that of Bahrain, where public protests were massive, and 39 percent of Saudis between the ages of twenty and twenty-four are unemployed.[8] Inflation has eaten away at the purchasing power of middle-class Saudis. Complaints about the deterioration of state-provided services and official corruption are as common in the kingdom as they are in other Arab countries.

## WHY SAUDI ARABIA REMAINED STABLE

The relative calm of the kingdom during the Arab upheavals is not because there are no reasons to protest. Rather, four factors contributed to the stability of the Saudi regime in this time of enormous regional change.

## BUYING LOYALTY

First is money. The Saudi rulers, in two decrees in February and March 2011, committed to spending nearly $130 billion over the next several years on their citizens. The biggest commitment was in housing (more than half the total spending), with a promise to build five hundred thousand homes over the next five years and to vastly increase the availability of state loans for home purchases. There were also immediate payouts: a one-time bonus equivalent to two months' salary for government employees, military personnel, and retirees with the largest private-sector employers following suit; the introduction of unemployment benefits; an increase in the minimum wage for the vast majority of Saudis in the workforce who are employed by the state or parastatal enterprises; a continuation of the 5 percent (approximate) inflation allowance to state salaries; and the creation of more than sixty thousand new public sector jobs.[9]

Unlike Egypt, Syria, Tunisia, Yemen, or even Bahrain, Saudi Arabia had the money in the bank to fund a massive increase in state payouts during the crisis. (Libya had the money, but Qaddafi was not adroit enough to use it in a timely manner.) It has had it because oil prices have been so high for the past several years. The Saudi Arabian Monetary Agency, the country's central bank, had $481 billion in foreign assets on hand in May 2011, more than enough to cover the new spending programs.[10] Even with the new financial obligations, the break-even price of oil—the price the Saudis need to meet their fiscal obligations—remains below the market price.[11] At least in the short term, the Saudis will have plenty of money at hand to deflect social and political pressures.

## DEPLOYING LOYAL AND WELL-TRAINED SECURITY FORCES

The second reason for the relative stability of Saudi Arabia in a season of Arab uprisings is the political reliability and deployment of its security services. The most important internal security forces—the police, secret police, and special forces under the control of the Ministry of Interior and the National Guard, commanded for decades by the king and now by one of his sons—are politically reliable. These forces are recruited disproportionately (though not exclusively) from tribes and areas the regime sees as particularly loyal. A combination of these units was deployed in the Eastern Province during protests among the Shia population there in February and March 2011. They demonstrated both that they were willing to arrest and shoot demonstrators, thus deterring larger protests, and that they were well trained enough to avoid massively violent responses to peaceful protests that might have embarrassed the regime and escalated confrontations.[12] Security forces were conspicuously deployed all over Riyadh on March 11, 2011, when Internet activists called for a "day of rage" against the regime that met with almost no popular response at all.[13]

The Saudi security forces were not always such bulwarks of the regime. Air force pilots famously defected to Cairo in 1962 when they were called on to assist the monarchical regime in North Yemen against an Egyptian-backed military coup. Saudi Arabia has seen a number of failed coup attempts in the past, the most serious recent example in 1969. But now the Saudi rulers seem to have found a happy medium with their security forces. They are not so independent that they might, as the Tunisian and Egyptian armies did, usher out their political masters. Members of the ruling family play important roles, not just commanding the various forces, but also as officers in their upper ranks. There are enough divisions in the security forces—regular army, National Guard, Interior Ministry forces—that it would be difficult for them to coalesce against the regime. These divisions in other circumstances, such as a serious succession fight, could lead to internal violence in Saudi Arabia. But now they help the al-Saud regime control its security forces. On the other hand, the security forces are professional and well trained enough to avoid the collapse and fragmentation that the Yemeni and Libyan armies suffered during their recent political upheavals.

## MOBILIZING THE REGIME'S PATRONAGE NETWORKS

The third factor contributing to the stability of al-Saud rule is, for want of a better term, their networks. The Saudi political system is built on patronage, flowing from the top down through groups (tribes, clans, and important business families) and institutions (as varied as the religious establishment, the media, and sporting clubs) to a wide range of individuals. Many benefits accruing to Saudi citizens are now processed bureaucratically and come without the need for intermediation with the higher-ups. The old days, when one had to attend a prince personally to ask for a benefice, have not disappeared completely, but this practice makes up a much smaller percentage of the benefits bestowed by the state than it once did. However, the al-Saud still maintain those personal networks of patronage and communication, dispensing access to government and personal favors to their clients. When crisis comes, they mobilize those networks to support the regime.

Such was the case in 2011. The most important of these networks is the religious establishment. In every crisis the regime has faced since the founding of the modern Saudi state at the turn of the twentieth century, the Wahhabi clerics holding high positions in the state religious hierarchy have rallied to the colors. As early as February 4, 2011, even before calls for demonstrations in Saudi Arabia itself, Sheikh Abd al-Aziz Al al-Sheikh, the grand mufti, the highest religious official in the country, condemned the marches and demonstrations occurring in Arab countries as "destructive acts of chaos" plotted by the enemies of Islam that result in "the shedding of blood, the abuse of dignities, the stealing of money and life in fear and terror and error."[14] On March 6, in advance of the so-called day of rage, the Council of Senior Clerics, which is the highest body in the official religious establishment, issued a statement forbidding demonstrations.[15] It is not clear how many Saudis still pay attention to the state-appointed arbiters of religion, but it certainly does not hurt to have them on one's side.

The clerics were not the only network activated by the al-Saud in response to the crisis. In the days leading up to the day of rage, both the king and Prince Muhammad bin Fahd, the governor of the Eastern Province, met delegations of Saudi Shia notables in an effort to head off large-scale protest among the most restive element of the Saudi population.[16] Security measures were probably more important in keeping Shia protests limited on the day of rage, but the very public assertions by the Saudi rulers of their ties with important Shia citizens were a reminder of the benefits they can bestow on the community as well, tangibly demonstrated by the release of some Shia prisoners. The Saudi business community, one of the most important constituencies of the ruling family, agreed to match for their private-sector employees the bonuses and salary increases the king awarded to the public sector. This was done not by law but through a few hints dropped by members of the ruling family in the ears of important businessmen. In the end, the stability of any regime depends on its ability to tie the interests of a range of important groups to its perpetuation. The al-Saud, aided both by their historical ties to the Wahhabi movement, central Arabian tribes, and important families, and by their vast oil wealth, have been able to build and sustain a broad network of support in the country.

## THE REFORMERS' DIVIDE

The divisions among the groups and movements pressing for political change are the fourth factor contributing to stability in Saudi Arabia. It is more than interesting that the two major petitions issued by Saudi intellectuals and activists in the early months of 2011 called for similar reforms: an elected parliament with full legislative powers, the independence of the judiciary, greater freedom to establish civil society organizations, guarantees of freedom of expression, the release of political prisoners, and greater efforts to root out official corruption.[17] One of the petitions was signed by a number of leading liberals and the other by notable *salafi* Islamists.[18] (Both petitions had hundreds of signatures; some activists signed both. They are defined according to their best-known signatories.) This agreement reflects that, at least at the elite level, Saudi activists are beginning to overcome differences of sect, region, and ideology. That important *salafis* are calling for democratic reform is a substantial ideological shift.[19] None of this can be welcome to the al-Saud rulers. (And they have reacted by issuing much more stringent regulations regarding political speech and continuing to arrest activists.[20]) But, in the immediate term, that there still had to be two petitions is more important. Liberals and Islamists were unable to unite their efforts, despite many common goals, unlike their counterparts in other Arab countries.

In the wake of these petitions, two issues emerged that highlighted these ideological splits and thus served the regime's immediate interest in preventing a coalescing of potential opposition. On March 2, 2011, a group of *salafis* accosted the Saudi minister of information at the Riyadh Book Fair, a major event for Saudi intellectuals, demanding that books they considered insulting to Islam be removed from the premises and that women either leave the premises or cover themselves completely.[21] Prominent liberal newspaper columnists reacted with a campaign against the *salafis*, accusing them of dragging the country backward. Thus, in the lead-up to the day of rage called for by Internet activists and publicized by regional and international media, Saudi political activists were divided on issues of women's rights and freedom of speech.

In May and June 2011, a few brave Saudi women got behind the wheel of their cars and drove in a few Saudi cities. Some were arrested; some posted videos of their transgressions on YouTube. The event, limited as it was, got disproportionate attention from the Western media because of how preposterous the continued Saudi ban on women driving is.[22] But in the Saudi context, women's issues more generally, and the driving ban in particular, mobilize intense Islamist opposition. To the extent that Saudis are arguing about women driving and just which books do or do not insult Islam, they will not be able to coalesce around common political reform demands and pressure the government.

## CHALLENGES TO REGIME STABILITY

That the Saudi regime has been able to ride out the year of Arab upheaval does not mean that it is out of the woods in terms of its medium-term political stability. Three issues could spark political crises that might, given the right circumstances, lead activists to put aside their ideological, regional, and sectarian differences and press for real political change.

### RAPID ROYAL SUCCESSIONS

The October 2011 death of Crown Prince Sultan, long-serving minister of defense and designated successor to King Abdallah, raises once again the thorny issue of succession in the al-Saud family.[23] King Abdallah is eighty-eight years old. He spent three months recuperating from back surgery outside the country as the Arab upheavals of 2011 were developing, returning in late February 2011. In October, he had another back surgery. Prince Nayif, minister of the interior, became crown prince after Sultan's death. He is seventy-eight and has his own health problems. The possibility of a late-Soviet-style set of aging rulers, dying in quick succession, looms.[24]

Other members of their generation, the sons of the founding king still active in government, would likely take their turns in the top job: Prince Salman, the long-serving governor of Riyadh who was recently appointed defense minister, and Prince Muqrin, head of foreign intelligence. As long as a competent member of that generation is present, there would probably not be a serious competition for the position. The picture could change when the top job moves to the next generation. There, the number of potential claimants increases, and there is no precedent for how rulership will pass to the grandsons of the founder. That first generational change will benefit one or two important princes and sideline many more. That is when intrafamily disputes would be most likely to emerge. Internal disputes in the past have been times of great danger for al-Saud rule in Arabia.[25] Such disputes encourage the rivals to mobilize support in society, risking a wider politicization that the Saudis in more normal times try to avoid. They set the security forces against each other. They encourage outsiders to meddle. Although a succession fight would be very dangerous for the country, it is not likely to happen while members of the older generation are still in power, and thus not for some years.

## FISCAL SQUEEZE

The second potentially regime-threatening issue for the Saudis would be a severe drop in oil prices. They have lived through the ups and downs of the oil market since 1973, but a deep decline in oil prices in the medium to long term would present a serious challenge to the patronage basis of the system. The Saudis are squeezed between two troubling trends. The first is the substantial new fiscal obligations taken on by the government this year. Although some of these are one-time expenses (the largest of which is the commitment to increase the housing stock), others (such as more government jobs, higher salaries, and a new unemployment benefit) are recurring. Saudi demographic trends mean that there will be more and more citizens who will need education, jobs, and subsidies over time. If the past is any indication, it is unlikely that Saudi defense spending will decrease while domestic spending demands grow. Fiscal pressures will thus increase over time. The second trend affects the revenue side of the Saudi government budget. Oil accounts for the overwhelming majority of Saudi revenues. But Saudi Arabia is consuming domestically larger and larger amounts of the oil it produces, reducing the quantity of oil available for export. Domestic oil consumption is heavily subsidized, encouraging a growing population to use more and more of it.

A thorough—and thoroughly troubling for Saudi decision-makers—examination of this squeeze was published by Jadwa Investment, a Saudi private investment firm, in July 2011.[26] They estimate that the government will have to run budget deficits from 2014, even if oil prices stay around their current level, with those deficits becoming substantial in the 2020s. By 2030, the break-even price of oil for the Saudis to meet their obligations will be over $300 per barrel.

The Jadwa analysis is not about the near term. The Saudis have plenty of money in the bank to handle their short-term needs, even if oil prices were to drop below $80 per barrel. In May 2011, net foreign assets held by the government and its various agencies exceeded $560 billion.[27] They can ride out an oil market crash over the next five years, were one to occur. There are also a number of assumptions in the analysis that might not pan out. Saudi Arabia might develop alternative sources for domestic energy consumption, such as nuclear and natural gas. It might adopt a more rational pricing strategy for energy, despite the political difficulties, and reduce the rate of consumption growth. But the country cannot sustain its current trajectories of government spending and energy consumption over the next twenty years. Something will have to give. A more rational fiscal course, involving either reduced government spending or systematic taxation of the citizenry or both, would challenge the bases of the oil state the al-Saud family has built since the early 1970s, with uncertain political consequences.

### HIGH YOUTH UNEMPLOYMENT

A final issue confronting the regime has less specific but still serious consequences for its longer-term stability—unemployment.[28] Saudi Arabia suffers from serious youth unemployment issues, as mentioned earlier, but unemployment rates drop dramatically for Saudis over thirty. Given that nearly two-thirds of Saudis are under the age of thirty, however, one wonders whether those relatively positive job numbers for the thirty-somethings can be sustained over time. The problem is not that the Saudi economy cannot generate private-sector jobs. On the contrary, between 2005 and 2009, more than 2.2 million jobs were created in the Saudi private sector. But over 90 percent of them went to expatriates. In both 2007 and 2008, more than one million work visas were issued. Saudis hold fewer than 10 percent of the total private-sector jobs in the country.[29]

The Saudi private sector prefers to hire expatriates. Except at the highest level of jobs, they work for smaller salaries than Saudi counterparts and are easier for employers to control. They frequently come with good English-language skills and degrees from respected educational systems in other Arab countries and South Asia. Saudi nationals themselves tend to want to work for the government because of its higher salaries and shorter working hours. Anecdotal evidence of younger Saudis being willing to forgo private sector employment and wait for years for a government job to come open for them is substantial. Breaking this syndrome would require decisive government steps to raise the cost of foreign labor for Saudi employers, but Saudi rulers have been unwilling to impose those costs on one of their most important constituencies. Past efforts at Saudization of the private-sector labor market have all failed to change this dynamic.

## A MISSED OPPORTUNITY FOR REFORM

None of these issues—succession, the fiscal squeeze, unemployment—presents an immediate threat to regime stability. They are medium- to long-term challenges. But they will be faced in a political atmosphere both domestically and regionally changed by the events of 2011. Although Saudis did not demonstrate in large numbers, they followed regional events closely. They are as wired up as any Arab population, more so than most. The clear sign from the 2011 petitions that liberals, Shia, and *salafis*, though divided on many issues, are coalescing around a demand for an elected parliament should not be ignored. The regime can deflect these pressures and play divide-and-rule among these groups, but it cannot change the momentum on the issue.

The al-Saud are well positioned now to deal with their problems. Enough of the older generation of princes remains able to set a succession pattern that would be accepted by the generation of the grandsons of Abd al-Aziz. (The Allegiance Council, set up in 2006, with representatives from each line of male heirs of the founding king, might be a step in this direction.[30]) The Saudi economy is healthy enough, after years of high oil prices and a growing role for the private sector, that longer-term issues of subsidies and taxes could be tackled. A change in government policy on foreign labor could help equalize the cost of foreign and local labor. All these steps require political will—the willingness to impose costs on clients and possibly alienate some sectors of society—for the longer-term welfare of the country as a whole.

Not faced with an immediate need to address any of the issues, it is more likely that the leadership will simply kick them down the road.

Given the demonstration of their political stability as states around them were engulfed by protest, the al-Saud could even preempt the growing convergence between more liberal and more *salafi* activists by introducing elections to the Consultative Council. However, the more likely lesson they will take from the year of Arab upheaval is that their system is working and there is no need for change. This will not lead to short-term instability, but it does mean a missed opportunity for managed political reform.

# Saudi Regional Policy in the Wake of the Arab Upheaval

If Saudi Arabia is the leader of the counterrevolution against the Arab Spring, it is time to rethink the definitions either of leadership or of counterrevolution. The Saudis were certainly counterrevolutionary in Bahrain, where they sent troops in March 2011 to bolster the uncompromising faction of the al-Khalifa ruling family in the face of massive public protests and demands for political reform. They were pained by the fall of their ally Mubarak in Egypt and more than a bit put out by U.S. policy toward Mubarak in his final days, but they could do little to save him.[31] They sought to support fellow monarchs in Morocco and Jordan by throwing geographical designations to the wind and inviting them to join the Gulf Cooperation Council (GCC) in May 2011, with financial support more than implied in that invitation.[32] Since the invitation, Muhammad VI of Morocco has supported constitutional change in a more democratic direction, having the prime minister come from the leading parliamentary party rather than be appointed at the king's discretion, and Abdallah II of Jordan has made noises about doing the same, though he has not yet followed through.[33] If Saudi patronage was supposed to swing those monarchs against political reform, it does not seem to be doing the job.

Riyadh took the lead in putting together a GCC plan for regime transition in Yemen aimed at easing President Saleh out of power. The Saudis backed the NATO-supported revolt in Libya that overthrew Qaddafi. In August 2011, they withdrew their ambassador from Syria, signaling their rejection of Assad's brutal crackdown on the protests there, and King Abdallah publicly called on Damascus to stop "the killing machine."[34] Aside from Bahrain, it is difficult to see where the Saudis have successfully stymied political change or political reform during this year of Arab upheavals. In some cases, they openly supported regime change.

## *THE SAUDI LOSING STREAK*

The better way to understand Saudi regional foreign policy is in terms of its contest for influence with Iran. Since 2003, when Iraq became a playing field rather than a player in regional politics, the Saudis found themselves the only Arab power with the means to check Iranian regional ambitions. After a brief period of trying to accommodate Iran (for instance by inviting President Mahmoud Ahmadinejad to Riyadh in March 2007), the Saudis have pursued a policy of balancing against, and rolling back where possible, Iranian influence in the Arab world.[35] For example, the high-profile (publicized by the Saudis in their own and the international media) Saudi military actions against the Huthi rebels in Yemen in November 2009, with air and artillery attacks by Saudi forces across the Yemeni border aimed at clearing the Huthis from the border area, were portrayed by Riyadh as an effort to curtail Iranian influence in Yemen.[36] The Saudis claimed victory against Iran in Yemen, as tenuous as that claim may have been, because they had suffered so many setbacks recently in their competition with Iran elsewhere. The three major areas in which Riyadh confronted Tehran were Iraq, Lebanon, and Palestine, and in all three it came up short.

### *IRAQ*

In Iraq, the Saudis' efforts to isolate Prime Minister Nouri al-Maliki and promote the fortunes of his major rival, Iyad Allawi, failed. They could not prevent Maliki from winning a second term as prime minister after the 2010 elections, despite Allawi's Iraqiyya Party's winning a few more seats than Maliki's State of Law Party. Iran was able to broker a deal between Maliki and its Shia allies in the National Iraqi Alliance (primarily the Sadrists and the Islamic Supreme Council of Iraq), giving Maliki the upper hand in the months-long stalemate over forming a government. Moreover, the Iraqi Awakening, or Sons of Iraq, movement that developed among Iraqi Sunnis to combat the influence of al-Qaeda in Iraq and cooperate with U.S. forces against the group has weakened and fragmented in recent years. The Awakening was an ideal vehicle for Saudi support in Iraq—Sunni, Arab, leery of Maliki, and opposed to Iranian influence in Iraq but also opposed to al-Qaeda—and received some amount of Saudi support. Saudi Arabia continues to refuse to deal with Maliki and there is no Saudi ambassador in Baghdad. Iranian influence in Iraq clearly outweighs Saudi influence.

## LEBANON

In Lebanon, Saudi Arabia supported the March 14 coalition and the Sunni political movement of slain former prime minister Rafiq al-Hariri and his son Saad against Iranian ally Hezbollah and its March 8 coalition. Despite March 14's electoral victories in 2005 and 2009, Hezbollah demonstrated its continuing power by conducting its own foreign policy (most notably in the war with Israel in 2006) and using its military force to occupy downtown Beirut in 2008. In January 2011, March 14 lost its parliamentary majority, as some of its elements (most notably Druze leader Walid Jumblatt) joined with March 8. Hezbollah was able to unseat Saad al-Hariri from the prime ministership. Najib Miqati, a Sunni politician less allied to Saudi Arabia and more acceptable to Hezbollah, formed the new Lebanese government. Much as in Iraq in 2010, despite its ally having won the election, the Saudis lost out to Iran in the contest for political influence.

## PALESTINE

In Palestine, Saudi Arabia supports the Palestinian Authority government, centered on the Fatah movement and Palestinian president Mahmoud Abbas, in the West Bank against Hamas, which has looked more to Iran for regional support. In February 2007 King Abdallah tried to bring Fatah and Hamas together, brokering an agreement between the two that sought to smooth over the tensions generated after Hamas's victory in the 2006 Palestinian legislative elections. The Saudi-mediated deal broke down within months, with Hamas securing control over Gaza and the Fatah consolidating its control in the West Bank amid bloody clashes between the Palestinian factions.

# A MIXED RESPONSE TO ARAB UPHEAVALS

It is against this backdrop of regional policy failures that Saudi Arabia faced the Arab upheavals of 2011. As its most important Arab ally, Mubarak in Egypt, fell from power, it seemed that the Saudi losing streak in regional politics was reaching a dangerous level. Riyadh's first impulse was defensive: to maintain its own sphere of influence in Arabia itself with its GCC partners and in Yemen. This was partly geopolitical, but it was also about its own domestic regime security.[37] The Saudi commitment to its monarchical partners in the GCC is as much about preserving the regime type as it is about keeping Iranian (or other) influences out of those close neighbors. It is here that Saudi policy is truly counterrevolutionary. Sending troops to Bahrain and promising massive financial aid for the government, though justified by Saudi leaders as a response to what they described as Iranian-sponsored efforts to unseat the Bahraini regime, was about preserving a fellow monarch more than anything else.[38] Continued sectarian conflict in Bahrain has a spillover effect in Saudi Arabia, exciting opposition within the Shia community in the Eastern Province, but preservation of the Bahraini monarchical system, even at the expense of possible problems with their own sectarian minority at home, trumped all considerations for Riyadh. The al-Saud believe they can handle their own domestic situation; it is the region they worry about. The Saudis, through the GCC, also promised to support the sultan of Oman (who faced serious protests, but not nearly on the level of Bahrain) with a similar level of aid.[39] The apparently ad hoc and sudden invitation to Jordan and Morocco to join the GCC in May 2011 stems from the same desire to preserve monarchy as a regime type in the Arab world.

## YEMEN

Saudi policy toward Yemen is not tied up with the sensitive issue of monarchy and thus is more focused on maintaining Saudi geopolitical dominance in a neighboring state and minimizing security risks. The Saudis have had a checkered relationship with Yemeni president Ali Abdullah Saleh over the decades—supporting him strongly in the late 1970s and 1980s against his Soviet-supported rivals in South Yemen, excoriating him for his support for Saddam Hussein in the Gulf War of 1990–91, and backing the failed secessionist effort by the socialist leaders of the former South Yemen in 1994. By 2000, they seemed to have made an uneasy peace with Saleh, seeing him as better than the alternatives in the country. However, they were not linked to him ideologically or personally in the same way that they are with their monarchical neighbors.

Thus, when it became clear that he was losing his grip on power, the Saudis stepped in with a plan to manage a transition, supported by the United States.[41] The slippery Saleh seemed to agree a number of times to a transition, only to back out at the last minute, clearly trying the

Saudis' (and others') patience. When he was injured in a bomb blast in his compound in June 2011, the Saudis hosted him during his convalescence. Most analysts doubted that they would allow him to return, but in September 2011 he reappeared in Yemen. In late November, Saleh, sitting next to King Abdullah in Riyadh, finally agreed to the GCC plan to transfer power to his vice president. Whatever happens in Yemen, the Saudis are confident that they will be able to sustain their influence through their myriad ties with Yemeni political, military, and tribal leaders. Although they certainly will not encourage democracy in Yemen, they will live with it if it emerges. They will not send in troops, as they did in Bahrain, to try to prevent it.

### EGYPT, LEBANON, LIBYA, AND SYRIA

The Saudis have been much less aggressive outside of their immediate sphere. They bemoaned the fall of Mubarak but moved quickly to establish a relationship with the Supreme Council of the Armed Forces that replaced him, with a commitment of $4 billion in aid.[41] They seemed to back away from their intense involvement in Lebanon after the fall of the Saad al-Hariri government. They supported the revolt against Qaddafi in Libya, but only verbally, whereas other GCC states, such as Qatar and the United Arab Emirates, contributed militarily to the effort. Most important, they wavered for months as demonstrations in Syria against the Assad regime escalated. Their inherent fear of regional instability held them back from supporting regime change against Iran's most important Arab state ally. Only in August 2011 did they publicly break with Assad.

## THE SOURCES OF SAUDI INFLUENCE

Saudi influence in the Arab world is normally exercised behind the scenes. Their military deployment into Bahrain is an exception to their modus operandi. Money is one key to Saudi regional influence. When it goes to governments, usually some evidence is left in the public record. When it goes to nongovernmental groups, it is much harder to find out about it. Thus, it is entirely possible that Saudi money, governmental or private or both, is going to the Syrian opposition to Assad, to elements of the Libyan opposition that overthrew Qaddafi, and to political groups in Egypt who competed in the November 2011 parliamentary elections.[42] It would not be surprising. But no evidence in the public record suggests that the Saudis are backing any of those groups financially at this time.[43]

Another element of Saudi influence in the broader Arab world is ideological. Riyadh has for decades promoted Islam generally and its own specific interpretation of Islam, Wahhabism or, as it is more commonly known in the Arab world, *salafism* (Arabic *salafiyya*—the imitation of the pious ancestors, the *salaf*, of the early generations of Islam). They mobilized Islam ideologically against the Arab nationalism of Gamal Abdul Nasser and the Baath Party of Syria and Iraq in the 1950s and 1960s, supporting the Muslim Brotherhood in particular as a counterweight to secular nationalists and leftists. After the great oil boom of the 1970s, the Saudis established numerous international, official governmental, and nongovernmental organizations to propagate the *salafi* version of Islam. They played an important role in the growth of the *salafiyya* throughout the region, to the point that *salafi* groups are playing an increasingly important role in the politics of most Arab states, most notably now in Egypt.

## SALAFISM: A DOUBLE-EDGED SWORD

That the Saudi role in the regional growth of *salafism* is unquestioned does not mean that Saudi Arabia can dictate political stances to *salafi* political groups or other Islamists. Their decades-long patronage of the Muslim Brotherhood did not help them during the first Gulf War, when most Brotherhood groups condemned their policy of inviting U.S. troops to the country and opposed the war against Iraq. Their support of the Arab volunteers in the jihad against the Soviet Union in Afghanistan in the 1980s was a major factor in the development of al-Qaeda, which took *salafi* ideas and turned them against the Saudi rulers. In the current Arab upheavals, the Saudi rulers cannot be comforted by the interesting development among some *salafis* in their thinking about democracy. Support for an elected legislature in Saudi Arabia by some notable *salafi* activists marks an important turn in domestic *salafi* political thought, away from their previous rejection of electoral democracy as un-Islamic. The growth of *salafi* democratic activism in Egypt is a mixed blessing for the Saudi rulers.[44] Egyptian *salafis* would most probably support close relations with Saudi Arabia, but the idea of active *salafi* participation in democratic politics is a disturbing precedent for a regime that has justified its lack of democracy by its interpretation of Islam.

So the Saudis cannot turn *salafism* on and off as their interests dictate, either at home or abroad. It would be a mistake to attribute *salafi* political strength in Egypt or Pakistan, for example, simply to Saudi machinations that, with enough U.S. pressure, can be brought to an end. But one element in current Saudi regional foreign policy that Riyadh can and should be discouraged from pursuing is strengthening sectarian identities and sectarian confrontation. The Saudis have made a conscious decision to increase the salience of the Sunni-Shia divide since the beginning of the Arab upheavals, to increase support for their allies, and to isolate Iran and its allies in the Arab world. The Saudi press depicted events in Bahrain as part of an Iranian effort to encourage Shia revolutions throughout the Arab world.[45] The mufti of Saudi Arabia, in response to a question about Iranian influence in the Gulf, said that "their whole history indicates their malice and hatred toward Islam and toward the Sunnis."[46] Sectarianism is an enduring reality in the eastern Arab world; the Saudis did not invent it. But they are clearly trying to stoke it now.

Raising the sectarian temperature around the region might help the Saudis mobilize domestic and regional support against Iran and its allies in the short term, but only at a serious cost. It makes movement toward compromise and effective governance in Iraq even less likely than it is now. It encourages conflict and discourages dialogue in Bahrain, where the U.S. 5th Fleet has its headquarters. It pushes Arab Shia politicians and groups toward Iran, offering the Iranians even more influence in Arab countries with large Shia populations. Sectarian tensions also help fuel *salafi* jihadist extremism, represented by al-Qaeda, because anti-Shiism is a strong element of the *salafi* extremist agenda. In such an atmosphere of regional tension, crises are more likely to spin out of control, increasing the chances of renewed civil wars in a number of Arab states and of direct Arab-Iranian confrontation that could drag the United States into another armed conflict in the Middle East.

# Saudi-U.S. Relations

U.S. analysts tend to not only exaggerate both Saudi domestic fragility and Saudi regional power but also exaggerate the level of tensions in the Saudi-U.S. relationship whenever differences between the two countries emerge. A Saudi watcher at an important Washington think tank declared recently that "U.S.-Saudi relations are in crisis."[47] A former high-ranking official on Middle East policy in the Clinton administration contended that the Saudis now see the Obama administration as a threat to their domestic security.[48] The *Los Angeles Times* spoke of the "rivalry that has erupted across the Middle East this year between Saudi Arabia and the United States, longtime allies that have been put on a collision course" by the Arab upheavals.[49] Without question, Washington and Riyadh have been at cross-purposes on some recent issues, most notably Mubarak's fall and the Saudi intervention in Bahrain. But talk of crisis and collision course is misleading. If the Saudi-U.S. relationship could withstand the real crises of the past—the oil embargo of 1973–74, the fallout of the 9/11 attacks—then the current differences are hardly enough to sever the tie.

That is certainly what the Saudis say.[50] Actions by Washington and Riyadh support the view that, despite tensions, there is no crisis in the relationship. Plans are proceeding for the United States to sell Saudi Arabia $60 billion in arms over the coming years. U.S. advisers are helping the Saudi Interior Ministry build a 35,000-man "special facilities security force" to protect Saudi oil installations.[51] Intelligence cooperation on counterterrorism continues at the highest levels. Washington and Riyadh have coordinated the efforts to manage a transition of power in Yemen. Both countries continue to see Iranian regional ambitions as a serious threat to their interests.

# THE SHIFT TO A
# TRANSACTIONAL RELATIONSHIP

But those who talk of a crisis in the relationship are on to something, even if they exaggerate the consequences. The geopolitical foundation of the post–World War II Saudi-U.S. relationship was a shared view of the Cold War and U.S. development of the Saudi oil industry. The latter changed fundamentally in the 1970s, when the Saudis assumed decision-making power on oil questions. U.S. companies are now customers, consultants, and occasionally partners in Saudi oil ventures, but the Saudis run their own oil policy. The most important growth markets for their energy exports are to their east, in South and East Asia, not to their west. As a result, their foreign policy focus is shifting in that direction. The end of the Cold War removed the common global foe that brought the two sides together and led to cooperation not just in the Middle East, but also in Africa, South Asia, Europe, and Latin America.

Saudi Arabia and the United States still have common interests on a number of issues, but the idea that they would automatically be on the same side in an international crisis (an exaggeration even at the time) ended with the Cold War. U.S. policymakers need to put aside the idea that they can go to the Saudis for help with issues as they arise and expect them to respond positively simply because the request is coming from Washington. Now the relationship is better characterized as transactional, each side seeking specific benefits from the other through cooperation on various issues, but with no assumption that they will line up together on the next issue that comes up.[52] That is certainly how one important Saudi recently depicted the situation. Prince Turki al-Faisal, former head of Saudi foreign intelligence and former ambassador to the United States, wrote in a *Washington Post* op-ed that U.S. opposition to the Palestinians' UN bid for recognition would lead Riyadh to pursue "policies at odds with those of the United States" toward Iraq, Yemen, and Afghanistan.[53] (Saleh's surprise return to Yemen from Saudi Arabia in late September 2011 might have been one such policy.) From now on, trade-offs will characterize the relationship more than a common worldview.

In this new transactional environment, how should the United States conduct its relations with Saudi Arabia? With less sensitivity about differences of opinion than in the past, but with a continuing awareness that a decent relationship with Riyadh is better for U.S. interests than dysfunctional competition. The United States should not pull its punches, rhetorical or practical, when its preferences differ from those of Saudi Arabia. Both U.S. and Saudi policymakers will adapt to living with wide and sharp differences on various issues. On Bahrain, for example, the United States should push for political reform and sectarian reconciliation, because it has no interest in maintaining a major military base in an unstable country, even though Saudi Arabia is backing the hardliners in the Bahraini ruling family. If Washington thinks democratic reform is the right policy for the Arab world, that the Saudis disagree should not matter a whit in the conduct of U.S. regional policy. U.S. officials can raise domestic reform issues in Saudi Arabia itself, publicly, though they should not expect much from the Saudis in response.

The recognition that Washington and Riyadh will differ on a number of issues and should thus not worry about a public airing of differences is important, but it cannot be the only element of the bilateral relationship. To best advance U.S. interests in the Middle East in the context of a transactional relationship with Saudi Arabia, the United States needs to prioritize those interests. It needs to speak consistently, across the various government agencies that have dealings with the Saudis, about the two or three top U.S. goals in the relationship. If the United States goes to the Saudis with a laundry list of desiderata, it is unlikely to get much beyond the first few items. If different U.S. agencies put forward different agendas in their dealings with the Saudis, Riyadh will simply pick and choose.

Maximizing U.S. leverage in the bilateral relationship requires a consistent U.S. focus on its most important priorities and all high-ranking officials working from the same playbook. The kind of incoherence exhibited in the spring of 2011, when the State Department was criticizing Saudi Arabia for its policy toward Bahrain while the secretary of defense, in his April visit to Riyadh, did not even raise the issue of Bahrain, should end.[54] What should those priorities be? They should be issues that are central to U.S. interests because it makes little sense wasting a transaction on a side concern. They should be things that one can reasonably expect to achieve, that the Saudis would not see as counter to their basic interests, and that the United States can deliver on as well.

# NONPRIORITY ISSUES

By those standards, a few issues that observers highlight in their critiques of the relationship should not make the top priorities list.

## CHANGING SAUDI DOMESTIC POLITICS

Since the 9/11 attacks, calls on Washington to make democratic political reform and even religious reform the centerpiece of the U.S.-Saudi dialogue have been numerous.[55] The merits of such a position from a moral perspective aside, it is a nonstarter with Riyadh. The Saudi leadership just weathered the Arab Spring by relying on their time-tested formula of oil money patronage, tough security policies, and a strong relationship with the Wahhabi religious establishment. They are not likely to change what for them has been a successful strategy of regime survival, no matter how many Americans tell them to do so. Rhetorical U.S. commitment to democratization in the region as a whole is not something the Saudis like, but they cannot do much about it. However, if the United States makes domestic political change in Saudi Arabia the centerpiece of the bilateral relationship, there is no future for it.

Washington also needs to be cautious in its approach to the ultimate domestic political issue in Saudi Arabia—succession in the ruling family. It is something about which the United States can do nothing practical, aside from urging all the parties to settle matters quickly and harmoniously. Any effort to affect the internal workings of the al-Saud family would undoubtedly backfire. The United States has limited experience in these kinds of endeavors, mostly negative. Its ability to pick the "right" candidate is questionable. (Most U.S. "experts" on Saudi Arabia twenty years ago thought the current king was a conservative, if not retrograde, anti-American character, indicating how wrong such conventional wisdom can be.) It would alienate most of the players in the game and thus most likely work against the favored candidate. Efforts by this or that ambitious prince to involve Washington on his side in such a situation should be resolutely resisted, and the prince told that the United States will not only not support individual candidates against others but will also oppose efforts to involve other foreign parties in the contest. Best to let the al-Saud work out their own issues and be ready to work with the leadership that emerges.

## SOLVING THE ARAB-ISRAELI CONFLICT

The issue of resolving the Arab-Israeli conflict, a hardy perennial, emerges from the Saudi side whenever there is a regional crisis.[56] Undoubtedly, progress in the Arab-Israeli arena would benefit regional stability and remove an irritant in Saudi-U.S. relations. One of the biggest crises in the relationship, the oil embargo of 1973–74, stemmed from an Arab-Israeli war. A more active U.S. policy on the peace process could be part of a transaction with the Saudis on other issues if Washington wants to move in that direction. But Saudi Arabia has lived with the close U.S. relationship with Israel for decades. The Saudis have not liked it, but they have not allowed it to disrupt cooperation with the United States on a range of issues. It would be a mistake to think that Saudi cooperation with the United States on matters of common interest depends on Arab-Israeli progress and equally a mistake to think that the tensions in the bilateral relationship would all disappear if Washington could produce a Palestinian-Israeli settlement.

## OIL PRICES

There is no denying that oil has been the center of the bilateral relationship since the outset of America's Middle East adventures. The United States cares about Saudi Arabia because it is the world's largest oil exporter, has the largest spare capacity of oil production in the world, and sits in a region that holds 60 percent of the world's known conventional oil reserves. U.S. presidents like the idea that, if gasoline prices were to get too high, they could call upon the Saudi king to moderate them. But, as Saudi revenue demands have grown and will continue to grow, given the fiscal commitments its government took on this year, Saudi Arabia is no longer the "price moderate" of past years. It needs high oil prices, higher than most Americans would like, to meet its domestic revenue needs.

The Saudis, because of their vast reserves, have a greater interest than other producers, such as Iran and Venezuela, in preventing prices from reaching levels that would spur conservation and the development of alternative fuels. Thus, in June 2011, in the wake of an acrimonious Organization of Petroleum Exporting Countries (OPEC) meeting, they raised oil production to moderate prices.[57] But they did this for their own reasons, not as a favor to the United States. U.S. policymakers should consult with the Saudis on oil issues, to be sure, but not make them the center of bilateral transactions. Riyadh will not bring prices down as far as most Americans would want, no matter what the offer. They will act on their own, in their own interest, to prevent prices from getting too high in their view. They will do this without an American quid pro quo, so there is no need to offer one.

## PRIORITY ISSUES

The priorities of the United States in the bilateral relationship should be regional security, counterterrorism, and nonproliferation. These three issues form a coherent whole and should be presented by U.S. interlocutors to Saudi officials as such. U.S. and Saudi interests on these issues generally align, making the forging of successful and mutually advantageous transactions more likely than in other issue areas.

### REGIONAL SECURITY

Regional security involves containment of Iranian ambitions and, where possible, rollback of Iranian influence in the Arab world. Saudi Arabia will certainly agree to that. But the United States needs to hammer away in every meeting with the Saudis that a number of recent Saudi policies are working against that shared goal. Saudi stoking of sectarian tensions pushes Arab Shia toward Iran. It increases domestic political tensions in Iraq, Kuwait, Bahrain, Lebanon, and even Saudi Arabia, raising the risk of upheavals that could destabilize the region further. The Saudis will argue that their move into Bahrain saved the country from falling into Iran's sphere of influence. U.S. officials need to counter that position; without a political solution to Bahrain's problems, Iran will be able to meddle there with impunity. A political solution in Bahrain is critical to the long-term security of the U.S. naval base there. At a minimum, the Saudi leadership has to signal its own media and its religious establishment to stop beating the sectarian drum. The United States should also push the Saudis to engage directly with the Iraqi government. Riyadh will be reluctant here, given its antipathy toward Prime Minister al-Maliki. But its current posture leaves Iran without a regional rival for influence in Baghdad. With the U.S. military withdrawal from Iraq proceeding, it is that much more important for the Saudis to engage Baghdad across the sectarian divide to provide an alternative.

Saudi fears of U.S. abandonment, or an imagined U.S.-Iranian deal that would leave them out in the cold, are exaggerated but real. They can be leveraged, but only in a most subtle way. As part of the regional security discussion, Washington needs to emphasize (as it repeatedly does) that withdrawal from Iraq does not mean withdrawal from the Gulf. The United States is not "abandoning" the Saudis and its other Gulf allies to Iranian hegemony by withdrawing troops from Iraq. But U.S. policymakers can share with the Saudis that domestic support for sustained U.S. security involvement in the Persian Gulf depends on having partners who cooperate. Without that, no U.S. administration can maintain U.S. commitments. The U.S. ability to play an effective and sustained role in regional security—something the Saudis want— depends on both the perception and the reality of allies who cooperate with the United States.

It is in the context of regional security that the United States should engage the Saudis on the prospects of a regime change in Syria. Both sides would benefit from Iran's loss of its major Arab state ally. Although Washington and Riyadh have different notions of what a post-Assad Syrian regime should look like, they share an interest in avoiding a civil war in Syria that could spill over into Lebanon and raise tensions on the Syrian-Israeli border.

## COUNTERTERRORISM COOPERATION

Cooperation in the counterterrorism field has improved dramatically in the decade since the 9/11 attacks and the mutual suspicions that followed. It remains for the United States to continue on this path, emphasizing to the Saudis the mutual threat that al-Qaeda and its various regional franchises pose. They understand, but also need to be reminded regularly that fanning the flames of sectarian tensions provides al-Qaeda with fertile ground for recruitment. U.S.-Saudi cooperation on Yemen is a major element of counterterrorism for both sides. U.S. officials should emphasize to their Saudi interlocutors that continued cooperation on Yemeni issues is part of the overall U.S. regional security and counterterrorism profile. The United States can be more cooperative on Yemeni issues and Syrian issues as they develop, if Saudi Arabia recognizes the counterproductive moves it has made on sectarian issues and on Iraq. This is an area where transactional diplomacy needs to be practiced more directly.

The persistent issue of funding coming from private sources in Saudi Arabia for jihadist and terrorist groups is an important part of the counterterrorism file. If the WikiLeaks documents are any indication, it is brought up regularly and prominently in Saudi-U.S. dialogues. Since 2008, a Treasury Department attaché office in the Riyadh embassy has been in regular contact with Saudi interlocutors in the Ministry of Interior, the Saudi Arabian Monetary Agency, the Ministry of Finance, intelligence units, and the Ministry of Foreign Affairs on the issue. The embassy reports significant progress on restricting al-Qaeda's ability to raise funds in the country, "now in its weakest state since 9/11." But Riyadh only recently focused attention on fundraising by groups that do not directly threaten Saudi security, like the Taliban, Lashkar-e-Taiba, and Hamas. Saudi moves against fundraising by these groups "remains almost completely dependent" on U.S. ability to "provide actionable intelligence to our Saudi counterparts."[58] The Saudis appreciate their intelligence relationship with the United States. U.S. diplomats already make clear that continued improvement of Saudi performance on this issue is essential to the ongoing relationship. That should continue.

If Saudi authorities do not act on intelligence leads from the United States on terrorist financing in a reasonable time, Washington should not hesitate to move itself, publicly, against Saudi citizens who are funding al-Qaeda and other jihadist groups through its own legal system and international legal channels. This should be a last resort, because the Saudi government has demonstrated in recent years that it now shares the American view of these groups as a serious threat. But it should be used when necessary. Naming and shaming such individuals will put pressure on the Saudi government, even within their own public opinion, to take harsher steps. In this, the United States would only be acting on principles that the Saudis have publicly adopted.

## NUCLEAR NONPROLIFERATION

The Saudis share the U.S. concern about the Iranian nuclear program. Their worries about Iran are so intense that they have signaled in numerous ways that—without saying it directly—they would feel it necessary to obtain their own nuclear deterrent if faced with an Iranian nuclear capacity.[59] The United States needs to emphasize to Riyadh that, given the vital U.S. and world interest in the free flow of oil from the Persian Gulf region, an Iranian nuclear breakout would lead to a redoubling of the U.S. security commitment to its regional allies, not to a U.S. withdrawal from the region. At the same time, Washington needs to make clear to the Saudis that a proliferation decision by them would fundamentally change their relationship with the United States, destabilize the region, and ultimately reduce their own security. This is a sensitive issue, but requires frank talk because of its sensitivity. There should not be any room for misunderstanding. It is important that this issue be on the table now with Riyadh and not be postponed until a potential Iranian nuclear breakout, because decisions in Saudi Arabia would likely (and uncharacteristically) be made very quickly were Iran to cross the weapons threshold. Washington should make this counterproliferation argument part of every discussion with Saudi Arabia about U.S. assistance with the development of the Saudi civilian nuclear industry, something that the Saudis are seeking through a "123" nuclear agreement with the United States.[60]

Washington should also be willing to extend an explicit nuclear guarantee to the states in the Gulf as long as Saudi Arabia eschews its own nuclear option.[61] That guarantee would have even more credibility if it came with a UN Security Council resolution supporting it and with a NATO declaratory policy backing it. Such a powerful statement of international intent might, if made known to the Iranians, act as a deterrent to their own nuclear breakout. Only such strong signals of U.S. commitment and international support could induce the Saudis to forgo acquiring their own nuclear force (probably from Pakistan, with which the Saudis have very close relations).

Unfortunately, Saudi Arabia and other Gulf states engage in some degree of magical thinking about the U.S. ability to prevent Iranian nuclear development. They would like the United States to "deal with" the Iranians on this issue but not do anything that might lead to Iranian counteraction against them.[62] Riyadh would, in all probability, support an American military strike against Iranian nuclear facilities, allowing U.S. forces access to Saudi facilities if needed (though without any publicity) and upping oil production to try to calm markets in the immediate aftermath, if Washington chose that path. But the Saudis would also blame the United States for any Iranian counterstrike and wonder about the value of the American security link if Iranian retaliation were serious. A steady U.S. policy of pressure on Iran, organized at the international level, regarding the nuclear issue might not be seen as enough by the Saudis, but is the only practical and long-term solution to this difficult situation. This needs to be emphasized repeatedly in bilateral discussion with the Saudis. The alternative of a military strike would most likely not end the Iranian nuclear pursuit, but rather only set it back. A strike would redouble Iran's political will to achieve a nuclear capability and lead to Iranian retaliation against Saudi Arabia and the Gulf states, not just militarily but also through political subversion over the longer term, most likely by stirring up Shia opposition.

# Conclusion

If U.S. policymakers keep these priorities front and center in their dealings with the Saudis, they will be able to take advantage of transactional diplomatic opportunities when the Saudis want something from Washington. If Riyadh would like to coordinate with Washington on regime change policy in Syria, Washington could ask for help on Iraq as part of its larger shared goal of regional stability. A new Saudi-U.S. initiative on Yemen could be made contingent on a Saudi promise to ratchet down the sectarian rhetoric. Saudi worries about Iran, voiced regularly to U.S. officials, should be met with the response that political dialogue across sectarian lines in Bahrain and Iraq would reduce the Iranian ability to meddle in the Arab world.

The United States needs Saudi Arabia, and Saudi Arabia needs the United States. Although the relationship no longer has its two historic bedrocks—the common Cold War perspective and the American operation of the Saudi oil industry—the two sides have numerous shared interests. If Washington understands that the Saudis are not fragile domestically, and that they have important but limited power to affect regional developments, it will have a realistic basis on which to deal with Riyadh. If Washington keeps its own priorities in the relationship clear and speaks with one voice about them to the Saudis, it should be able to realize those common interests with Saudi Arabia.

# Endnotes

1. The quote was in response to a query about congressional sentiment regarding a potential Saudi-American agreement on a civilian nuclear deal. Howard LaFranchi, "Obama Administration mulls India-style nuclear pact with Saudi Arabia," *Christian Science Monitor*, July 29, 2011, http://www.csmonitor.com/USA/Foreign-Policy/2011/0729/Obama-administration-mulls-India-style-nuclear-pact-with-Saudi-Arabia.
2. The Project on Middle East Political Science issued a compendium of short analytical articles on the country on August 9, 2011, many previously published on the Middle East Channel of ForeignPolicy.com, entitled "The Saudi Counter-Revolution," http://www.pomeps.org/2011/08/10/arab-uprisings-the-saudi-counter-revolution. See also Toby Jones, "Saudi Arabia's Regional Reaction," *Nation*, September 12, 2011, and Bruce Reidel, "Brezhnev in the Hejaz," *National Interest*, no. 115 (September/October 2011): "Riyadh has become the de facto leader of the counterrevolution in the Middle East."
3. Such a prediction was made by Abd al-Aziz's close confidant and English-language court historian. H. St. John B. Philby, "The New Reign in Saudi Arabia," *Foreign Affairs*, vol. 32, no. 3 (April 1954).
4. In June 1962, Robert Komer, a Kennedy administration National Security Council official, wrote to National Security Adviser McGeorge Bundy that "the staying power of the Saudi monarchy declines with every passing day." Cited by Rachel Bronson, *Thicker Than Oil: America's Uneasy Partnership with Saudi Arabia* (New York: Oxford University Press, 2006), p. 83.
5. Toby Jones, "High Anxiety," ForeignPolicy.com, March 23, 2011, http://mideast.foreignpolicy.com/posts/2011/03/23/high_anxiety; Karen Elliott House, "From Tunis to Cairo to Riyadh?" *Wall Street Journal*, February 15, 2011; Martin Indyk, "Amid the Arab Spring, Obama's Dilemma over Saudi Arabia," *Washington Post*, April 8, 2011: "The Saudi system is fragile."
6. The caricature of the Arab oil sheikh wrapping the gas pump hose around an American driver was a popular political cartoon subject during the 1973–74 oil embargo and has reappeared whenever gasoline prices rise. On post-9/11 charges that Saudi Arabia was responsible for the spread of Sunni Islamist extremism in the world, and thus ultimately responsible for the 9/11 attacks, see, for example, Robert Baer, *Sleeping with the Devil: How Washington Sold Our Soul for Saudi Crude* (New York: Crown Books, 2003); Dore Gold, *Hatred's Kingdom: How Saudi Arabia Supports the New Global Terrorism* (Washington: Regnery Publishers, 2003); Stephen Schwartz, *The Two Faces of Islam: The House of Saud from Tradition to Terror* (New York: Doubleday, 2002); and Laurent Murawiec, *Princes of Darkness: The Saudi Assault on the West* (Lanham, MD: Rowman & Littlefield, 2005). Murawiec used the phrase "kernel of evil" to describe Saudi Arabia in a briefing to the Pentagon's Defense Policy Board. Thomas Ricks, "Briefing Depicted Saudis as Enemies," *Washington Post*, August 6, 2002, p. 1.

7. One petition can be found at "A Declaration of National Reform," Saudi Reform, http://www.saudireform.com. The other petition was originally available at http://www.dawlaty.info, but that site is now inoperative.

8. Banque Saudi Fransi, "Saudi Arabia Economics: Employment Quandary," February 16, 2011, http://www.alfransi.com.sa/en/section/about-us/economic-reports. Although Saudi youth unemployment is high in this age group, it falls markedly over that demographic decade. The unemployment rate for Saudis age thirty to thirty-four is below 5 percent. Perhaps it is not the reality of youth unemployment that is politically destabilizing, but the realization that one's prospects will not soon improve.

9. For a concise description of these various plans, see Banque Saudi Fransi, "Saudi Arabia Economics: Strategy Shift," April 4, 2011, http://www.alfransi.com.sa/en/section/about-us/economic-reports.

10. Jadwa Investment, "Saudi Arabia's Coming Oil and Fiscal Challenge," July 2011, p. 11, http://www.jadwa.com/Research/store/Oil%20_%20fiscal%20challange%20-%20July%202011.pdf.

11. Jadwa Investment estimates the current break-even price at $84 per barrel; Banque Saudi Fransi at "about $80 per barrel." Jadwa Investment, "Saudi Arabia's Coming Oil and Fiscal Challenge," p. 1; Banque Saudi Fransi, "Saudi Arabia Economics: Strategy Shift," p. 5. The average price of Saudi crude is about midway between the two major benchmark prices used in oil trading, West Texas Intermediate and Brent. Jadwa Investment, "Saudi Arabia's Coming Oil and Fiscal Challenge," p. 14.

12. Neela Banerjee, "Saudi security forces break up protest in eastern city," *Los Angeles Times*, March 11, 2011; Michael Birnbaum, "Saudi Arabia seems quiet on planned 'Day of Rage,'" *Washington Post*, March 12, 2011. A local Shia activist website reported more casualties on the March 10 demonstrations in the Eastern Province (http://www.rasid.com/artc.php?id=43310).

13. Neela Banerjee, "Saudi Arabia 'day of rage' protest fizzles," *Los Angeles Times*, March 12, 2011.

14. Abd al-Aziz al-Atar, "mufti al-mamlaka: al-muthaharat khutut li-tafkik al-'umma," *al-Watan*, February 5, 2011, http://www.alwatan.com.sa/Local/News_Detail.aspx?ArticleID=40472.

15. "The correct way in Shariah (Islamic law) of realizing common interest is by advising, which is what the Prophet Muhammad (peace be upon him) established. . . . Reform and advice should not be via demonstrations and ways that provoke strife and division. This is what the religious scholars of this country in the past and now have forbidden." "Top Saudi Scholars Back Ban on Protests," *Khaleej Times* (Dubai), March 7, 2011, http://www.khaleejtimes.com/DisplayArticleNew.asp?xfile=/data/middleeast/2011/March/middleeast_March119.xml&section=middleeast.

16. Abeer Alam, "Protests Build Across Saudi Arabia," *Financial Times*, March 5, 2011.

17. These two petitions, along with the lists of signatories, were found at these websites: one, "A Declaration of National Reform," at http://www.saudireform.com, and the other at http://www.dawlaty.info, which is now inoperative. A third petition, voicing similar demands, signed by a number of younger activists, also appeared at this time (http://www.massdar.net/site/shownews.php?&nid=2556).

18. The term *salafi* refers to Islamist activists who are extremely scriptural in their interpretation of Islam and who advocate imitation of the early Muslims (the ancestors, *al-salaf* in Arabic) in social behavior (such as style of dress and personal appearance, including untrimmed beards). They are also referred to as Wahhabis, followers of the eighteenth-century Islamist activist Muhammad ibn Abd al-Wahhab, who made the original pact with Muhammad ibn Saud that began the alliance between this version of Islam and the al-Saud family's political fortunes.

19. Salman al-Awda is the most interesting case here. He was a fierce critic of the Saudi regime in the 1990s and spent some time in jail for his trouble. He rallied to the defense of the regime in the crisis after the 9/11 attacks, defending it against both its Western critics and al-Qaeda. He became something of a regime favorite and was given his own television show on the Saudi-owned Middle East Broadcasting (MBC) network, one of the Arab world's most important satellite channels. He signed the dawlaty.info petition and, on his website, strongly supported the Egyptian uprising against the Mubarak regime. (For an English translation of that statement, see Sheikh Salman al-Oadah, "Has Egypt's Hour Reckoning Come?" *Islam Today*, February 2, 2011, http://en.islamtoday.net/artshow-413-3937.htm.) As a result, his show, *Life Is a Word*, was canceled. "D. Salman Return: Missed Life is a Word but I did not lose trust in my God," *Islam Today*, February 24, 2011, http://islamtoday.net/salman/artshow-78-146578.htm.

20. Neil MacFarquhar, "Proposed law would mandate jail for critics of Saudi king," *New York Times*, July 22, 2011; "Saudi Arabia: Rights Activists, Bloggers Arrested," Human Rights Watch, May 3, 2011, http://www.hrw.org/news/2011/05/03/saudi-arabia-rights-activist-bloggers-arrested. For a surprisingly direct criticism of the new laws on freedom of speech by a Saudi, see this editorial cartoon in the May 2, 2011, edition of *al-Hayat*, http://ksa.daralhayat.com/ksaarticle/262066.

21. Muhammad Sa'ud and Abdallah al-Duhaylan, "muhtasibun yatahajimun 'ala wazir al-i'lam wa yahtajun 'ala al-'ikhtilat," *al-Hayat KSA*, March 3, 2011, http://ksa.daralhayat.com/ksaarticle/240320.

22. Caryle Murphy, "Women still can't drive in Saudi Arabia," *Global Post*, June 25, 2011, http://www.globalpost.com/dispatch/news/regions/middle-east/saudi-arabia/110624/women-driving-rights; Alexandra Sandels, "Women get in the driver's seat to defy ban," *Los Angeles Times*, June 28, 2011, http://articles.latimes.com/2011/jun/18/world/la-fg-saudi-women-drivers-20110618; Neil MacFarquhar and Dina Saleh Amer, "In a scattered protest, Saudi women take the wheel," *New York Times*, June 17, 2011, http://www.nytimes.com/2011/06/18/world/middleeast/18saudi.html.

23. This is the most closely held issue in Saudi Arabia. Members of the ruling family rarely if ever talk about it to outsiders, yet it is the subject of intense and constant gossip. Generally, "those who know do not talk and those who talk do not know," so one should be leery of any published material on the subject. The best, most recent scholarly treatment is Joseph A. Kechichian, *Succession in Saudi Arabia* (New York: Palgrave, 2001).

24. Karen Elliott House writes, "All this is reminiscent of the dying decade of the Soviet Union, when one aged and infirm Politburo chief succeeded another." She also reported that Prince Sultan suffered from cancer and Alzheimer's disease. Karen Elliott House, "From Tunis to Cairo to Riyadh?" *Wall Street Journal*, February 15, 2011.

25. The best scholarly account of the most recent period of al-Saud family strife is Sarah Yizraeli, *The Remaking of Saudi Arabia: The Struggle Between King Saud and Crown Prince Faisal* (Tel Aviv: The Moshe Dayan Center, 1997). A lively account is provided by Robert Lacey, *The Kingdom* (New York: Harcourt Brace Jovanovich, 1981).

26. Jadwa Investment, "Saudi Arabia's coming oil and fiscal challenge," July 2011, http://www.jadwa.com/Research/store/Oil%20_%20fiscal%20challenge%20-%20July%202011.pdf. One of the most troubling findings of the report is that, at current rates of consumption growth, Saudi Arabia will go from consuming 2.4 mbd of oil domestically in 2010 to consuming 6.5 mbd in 2030, losing the revenue that could have been gained from exporting that oil (pp. 18–21). A summary of the findings can be found at Robin M. Mills, "The Kingdom of Magical Thinking," ForeignPolicy.com, August 25, 2011, http://www.foreignpolicy.com/articles/2011/08/25/the_kingdom_of_magical_thinking.

27. Jadwa Investment, "Saudi Arabia's Coming Oil and Fiscal Challenge," July 2011, http://
    www.jadwa.com/Research/store/Oil%20_%20fiscal%20challange%20-%20July%20
    2011.pdf, p. 11.
28. A good, recent account of the problem is Ellen Knickmeyer, "Idle Kingdom,"
    ForeignPolicy.com, July 29, 2011, http://www.foreignpolicy.com/articles/2011/07/19/
    all_play_no_work.
29. Banque Saudi Fransi, "Saudi Arabia Economics: Employment Quandary," February
    16, 2011, pp. 1–3, http://www.alfransi.com.sa/en/section/about-us/economic-reports.
30. For a brief account of the establishment and function of this new, untested institution,
    see Robert Lacey, *Inside the Kingdom* (New York: Viking, 2009), pp. 268–70.
31. Adam Entous, Julian Barnes, and Jay Solomon, "U.S. Pressure on Mubarak Opens Rift
    with Arab Allies," *Wall Street Journal*, February 4, 2011, http://online.wsj.com/article/
    SB10001424052748704376104576122610828648254.html; David Kirkpatrick and
    David Sanger, "A Tunisian-Egyptian Link that Shook Arab History," *New York Times*,
    February 13, 2011, http://www.nytimes.com/2011/02/14/world/middleeast/14egypt-
    tunisia-protests.html?pagewanted=all.
32. Saudi Arabia has reportedly already provided Jordan, since the invitation, with $1.4
    billion in aid. Sean Yom, "Jordan Goes Morocco," ForeignPolicy.com, August 22, 2011,
    http://mideast.foreignpolicy.com/ posts/2011/08/19/jordan_goes_morocco.
33. On the Jordanian promise, see Sean Yom, "Jordan Goes Morocco," ForeignPolicy.
    com, August 22, 2011, http://mideast.foreignpolicy.com/ posts/2011/08/19/jordan_
    goes_morocco. On the Moroccan reforms, see Bourzou Daragahi, "Moroccan king
    proposes constitutional reforms," *Los Angeles Times*, June 18, 2011.
34. J. David Goodman, "Saudi Arabia Ramps Up Pressure on Syria," *New York Times*,
    August 8, 2011, http://www.nytimes.com/2011/08/09/world/middleeast/09saudi.html.
35. For an extended discussion of Saudi regional policy, see F. Gregory Gause, "Saudi
    Arabia's Regional Security Strategy," in Mehran Kamrava, ed., *International Politics of
    the Persian Gulf* (Syracuse: Syracuse University Press, 2011). It is in the context of this
    ongoing Saudi-Iranian battle for regional influence that the amateurish plot by Iranian
    operatives to assassinate the Saudi ambassador in Washington, revealed by the Justice
    Department in October 2011, should be understood. Whether the plot is actually
    connected to the top levels of the Iranian government or whether it was hatched in
    the fervid imagination of an Iranian-American on the make, caught up in an FBI
    sting operation, is not a question that can be answered definitively given the current
    evidence. But it makes perfect sense to a Saudi government that has been fighting Iran
    in the shadows for some time.
36. Jeffrey Fleishman, "Saudi fighter jets target rebels inside Yemen," *Los Angeles Times*,
    November 6, 2009, http://articles.latimes.com/2009/nov/06/world/fg-yemen6. For
    background on the Huthi rebellion, see International Crisis Group, Yemen: *Defusing the
    Saada Time Bomb*, Middle East Report No. 86, May 27, 2009, http://www.observatori.
    org/paises/pais_64/documentos/86_yemen___defusing_the_saada_time_bomb.
    pdf, pp. 2–4. For an example of how the Saudis portrayed this incident as part of their
    campaign against Iranian expansion in the Arab world, see the column by influential
    Saudi commentator Daud al-Shiryan in *al-Hayat*, "Yemen in confrontation with Iran,"
    August 20, 2009, http://international.daralhayat.com/internationalarticle/48895.
    The actual amount of Iranian support for the Huthi rebellion is unclear but probably
    limited. The International Crisis Group report cited quotes a Western diplomat in
    Yemen: "There is no clear evidence of Iranian involvement but small signs of a role by
    Iranian charitable organisations. Overall, however, the conflict appears chiefly fuelled
    by internal grievances" (p. 12).

37. The Saudi leadership tends to conflate its geopolitical contest with Iran with its own domestic regime security, because it sees Iran as not only competing for regional influence with Saudi Arabia but also trying to destabilize the Saudi regime domestically. In late August 2011, Prince Nayif, then the de facto number two in the ruling hierarchy, said that "we will continue to be a target for terrorists, who will continue to attempt to attack us, with support from other parties. Evil surrounds us from all sides." Later in the interview he said that one of the sources of that evil is "Iran and its targeting of the kingdom." "Saudi Arabia says it remains a target for terrorism," *Gulf Times*, August 30, 2011, http://gitm.kcorp.net/index. php?id=572083&news_type=Top&lang=en. This cartoon in the Saudi newspaper *al-Watan* on March 14, 2011, sums up the Saudi view, with an Iranian mullah aiming an arrow at a sturdy date palm labeled the kingdom, only to have the arrow run him through. See "Jihad Awartani," *al-Watan*, http://www.alwatan.com.sa/Caricature/Detail.aspx?CaricaturesID=1568.

38. An unnamed Saudi official told David Ignatius after the troop deployment, "We do not want Iran fourteen miles off our coast, and that is not going to happen." But a second Saudi official revealed the more important reason to Ignatius when he said "we're going in to keep a system in place." David Ignatius, "High Stakes over Bahrain," *Washington Post*, March 16, 2011, http://www.washingtonpost.com/opinions/high-stakes-over-bahrain/2011/03/15/AB7ykyZ_story.html.

39. "Gulf states launch $20 billion fund for Oman and Bahrain," Reuters, March 10, 2011, http://www.reuters.com/article/2011/03/10/us-gulf-fund-idUSTRE7294B120110310.

40. Abeer Allam and Roula Khalaf, "Saudis prepare to abandon Yemen," *Financial Times*, March 23, 2011; Iona Craig, "Yemen peace deal falters," *Los Angeles Times*, May 23, 2011.

41. "$4 billion in Saudi aid for Egypt," *Arab News*, May 22, 2011, http://www.arabnews.com/saudiarabia/article420017.ece.

42. There is a strong belief in Egypt that Saudi Arabia is supporting the newly emerged *salafi* political parties there. Noha El-Hennawy, "Military-Salafi relations in Egypt raise questions," *al-Masry al-Youm* (English), May 10, 2011, http://www.almasryalyoum.com/en/node/431100. The Saudi ambassador to Egypt denied reports in the Egyptian press that Saudi Arabia was providing billions of dollars in support to Egyptian *salafis*. Randa Abul Azm, "Saudi envoy to Egypt denies Kingdom offered *salafis* billions," *al-Arabiyya News*, August 1, 2011, http://www.alarabiya.net/articles/2011/08/01/160331.html.

43. Yemen is an exception here. Saudi financial support for tribes, groups, and individuals in Yemen is an open secret and Yemenis are usually willing to talk about it. See, for example, Robert Worth, "Yemen on the Brink of Hell," *New York Times Magazine*, July 20, 2011, where a tribal sheikh acknowledges that the Saudis pay him $2,500 per month.

44. Neil MacFarquhar, "Religious Radicals Turn to Democracy Alarms Egypt," *New York Times*, April 2, 2011, http://www.nytimes.com/2011/04/02/world/middleeast/02salafi.html?pagewanted=all.

45. A good example is the series of articles by Jasir al-Jasir, a columnist in the Saudi daily *al-Jazirah*, published on March 12–17, 2011, under the provocative title "The plans of the Safavid regime to destroy the Gulf states" (March 12–14) and "The plans of the Safavid regime to destroy the Arab states" (March 15–17). They are available online at http://www.al-jazirah.com.sa/writers/2011i.html.

46. Abdallah Al-Dani, "al-mufti al-'am: al-safawiyun al-majus haqidun 'ala ahl al-islam," *Ukaz*, April 15, 2011, http://www.okaz.com.sa/new/Issues/20110415/Con20110415412196.htm.

47. Simon Henderson, "Outraged in Riyadh," ForeignPolicy.com, April 14, 2011, http://www.foreignpolicy.com/articles/2011/04/14/outraged_in_riyadh.

48. Martin Indyk, "Amid the Arab Spring, Obama's Dilemma over Saudi Arabia," *Washington Post*, April 8, 2011, http://www.washingtonpost.com/opinions/amid-the-arab-spring-obamas-dilemma-over-saudi-arabia/2011/04/07/AFhILDxC_story.html.

49. Paul Richter and Neela Banerjee, "U.S.-Saudi rivalry intensifies," *Los Angeles Times*, June 19, 2011, http://articles.latimes.com/2011/jun/19/world/la-fg-us-saudis-20110619.

50. Bill Spindle and Margaret Coker, "The New Cold War," *Wall Street Journal*, April 16, 2011, http://online.wsj.com/article/SB100014240527487041164045762627441064838316.html: "Saudi officials say that despite the current friction in the U.S.-Saudi relationship, they won't break out of the traditional security arrangement with Washington."

51. Robert Burns, "US quietly expanding defense ties with Saudis," *Army Times*, May 19, 2011, http://www.armytimes.com/news/2011/05/ap-us-quietly-expanding-defense-ties-with-saudis-051911.

52. Former American ambassador to Saudi Arabia Chas Freeman suggested the term *transactional* to describe the current relationship.

53. Turki al-Faisal, "Veto a State, Lose an Ally," *New York Times*, September 11, 2011, http://www.nytimes.com/2011/09/12/opinion/veto-a-state-lose-an-ally.html.

54. Elisabeth Bumiller, "Defense Chief is on Mission to Mend Saudi Relations," *New York Times*, April 7, 2011, http://www.nytimes.com/2011/04/07/world/middleeast/07military.html.

55. One of the more recent iterations of this position, from someone who has stressed it for a decade now, can be found in Thomas Friedman, "Bad Bargains," *New York Times*, May 10, 2011, http://www.nytimes.com/2011/05/11/opinion/11friedman.html. In the wake of the killing of Osama bin Laden, he wrote, "I just wish it were as easy to eliminate the two bad bargains that really made that attack [9/11] possible, funded it and provided the key plotters and foot soldiers who carried it out. We are talking about the ruling bargains in Saudi Arabia and Pakistan, which are alive and well."

56. See also Turki al-Faisal, "Failed favoritism toward Israel," *Washington Post*, June 10, 2011, http://www.washingtonpost.com/opinions/palestinian-rights-wont-be-denied-by-the-united-states-and-israel/2011/06/07/AGmnK2OH_story.html: "There will be disastrous consequences for U.S.-Saudi relations if the United States vetoes U.N. recognition of a Palestinian state."

57. Ronald D. White, "Oil and gas prices fall as Saudi Arabia moves to increase output," *Los Angeles Times*, June 11, 2011, http://articles.latimes.com/2011/jun/11/business/la-fi-gas-prices-20110611.

58. Quotes taken from a U.S. embassy Riyadh cable dated February 12, 2010, "Scenesetter for Special Representative Holbrooke's February 15–16 Visit to Riyadh," Cablegate, http://www.cablegatesearch.net/cable.php?id=10RIYADH182&q=arabia%20saudi.

59. A leaked American diplomatic cable reported a lesser-ranking Saudi official telling American and other interlocutors that, if Iran obtained nuclear weapons, Saudi Arabia would do the same. See "US embassy cables: Saudi official warns Gulf states may go nuclear," *Guardian*, http://www.guardian.co.uk/world/us-embassy-cables-documents/189229. In a speech delivered at an RAF base in England in June 2011, Prince Turki al-Faisal hinted that an Iranian acquisition of nuclear weapons would lead Saudi Arabia to do the same, though he did not say so directly. A "senior official in Riyadh who is close to the prince" later confirmed to the *Guardian* that this was the message Prince Turki was sending. For the text of the speech, see "A Saudi National Security Doctrine for the Next Decade," SUSRIS, July 11, 2011, http://www.susris.com/2011/07/11/a-saudi-national-security-doctrine-for-the-next-decade-prince-turki-al-faisal/. For the

subsequent quote, see Jason Burke, "Riyadh will build nuclear weapons if Iran gets them, Saudi prince warns," *Guardian*, June 29, 2011, http://www.guardian.co.uk/world/2011/jun/29/saudi-build-nuclear-weapons-iran.

60. Howard LaFranchi, "Obama administration mulls India-style nuclear pact with Saudi Arabia," *Christian Science Monitor*, July 29, 2011, http://www.csmonitor.com/layout/set/print/content/view/print/400276.

61. This is not a new idea. See, for example, Bruce Riedel, "Iran-U.S.: After the Iranian Bomb," Center for Strategic Research, Institute for National Strategic Studies, National Defense University, September 30, 2011, http://www.ndu.edu/inss/docUploaded/RIEDEL_IRAN_US_CSR_REPORT.pdf. Secretary Clinton raised the possibility of such a strategy in public remarks in July 2009. Mark Langer and David E. Sanger, "Clinton Speaks of Shielding Mideast from Iran," *New York Times*, July 22, 2009, http://www.nytimes.com/2009/07/23/world/asia/23diplo.html.

62. WikiLeaks documents indicate that King Abdallah had, if not directly called for an American military strike on Iranian nuclear sites, at least indicated that he would not mind if it happened. See the April 2008 U.S. embassy report of a visit by General Petraeus and Ambassador Ryan Crocker to Saudi Arabia and "State's Secrets," *New York Times*, http://www.nytimes.com/interactive/2010/11/28/world/20101128-cables-viewer.html#report/iran-08RIYADH649.

# About the Author

F. Gregory Gause III is a professor and chair of the political science department at the University of Vermont. In 2009 and 2010, he was the Kuwait Foundation visiting professor of international affairs at Harvard University's Kennedy School of Government. He was previously on the faculty of Columbia University between 1987 and 1995, and was also the fellow for Arab and Islamic studies at the Council on Foreign Relations from 1993 to 1994. His scholarly articles have appeared in *Foreign Affairs, Foreign Policy, Security Studies, Middle East Journal*, and other journals and edited volumes. His most recent book is *The International Relations of the Persian Gulf*. He has testified on Gulf issues before congressional committees and has made numerous appearances on television and radio commenting on Middle East issues. Gause received his PhD in political science from Harvard University and his BA summa cum laude from St. Joseph's University in Philadelphia. He also studied Arabic at the American University in Cairo and Middlebury College.

# Advisory Committee for
## *Saudi Arabia in the New Middle East*

Odeh F. Aburdene
*OAI Advisors*

Jon B. Alterman
*Center for Strategic & International Studies*

Michael Barnett
*George Washington University*

Dwight Bashir
*U.S. Commission on
International Religious Freedom*

Christopher Boucek
*Carnegie Endowment for International Peace*

Ray Close

Charles G. Cogan
*Belfer Center for Science
and International Affairs*

Kristen S. Diwan
*American University*

Chas W. Freeman Jr.
*Projects International, Inc.*

Brian Katulis
*Center for American Progress*

Alan Larson
*Covington & Burling, LLP*

Thomas W. Lippman
*Middle East Institute*

Marc Lynch
*George Washington University
and Center for a New American Security*

Suzanne Maloney
*Brookings Institution*

Edward L. Morse
*Citigroup Global Markets, Inc.*

Richard W. Murphy
*Middle East Institute*

Daniel Pipes
*Middle East Forum*

Paul B. Stares, *ex officio*
*Council on Foreign Relations*

Christoph Wilcke
*Human Rights Watch*

Mona Yacoubian
*Henry L. Stimson Center*

# CPA Advisory Committee

Peter Ackerman
*Rockport Capital, Inc.*

Richard K. Betts
*Council on Foreign Relations*

Patrick M. Byrne
*Overstock.com*

Leslie H. Gelb
*Council on Foreign Relations*

Jack A. Goldstone
*George Mason University*

Sherri W. Goodman
*CNA*

General George A. Joulwan, USA (Ret.)
*One Team, Inc.*

Robert S. Litwak
*Woodrow Wilson International Center for Scholars*

Thomas G. Mahnken
*Paul H. Nitze School of Advanced International Studies*

Doyle McManus
Los Angeles Times

Susan E. Patricof
*Mailman School of Public Health*

David Shuman
*Northwoods Capital*

Nancy E. Soderberg
*University of North Florida*

General John W. Vessey, USA (Ret.)

Steven D. Winch
*Ripplewood Holdings, LLC*

James D. Zirin
*Sidley Austin, LLP*

# Mission Statement of the
# Center for Preventive Action

The Center for Preventive Action (CPA) seeks to help prevent, defuse, or resolve deadly conflicts around the world and to expand the body of knowledge on conflict prevention. It does so by creating a forum in which representatives of governments, international organizations, nongovernmental organizations, corporations, and civil society can gather to develop operational and timely strategies for promoting peace in specific conflict situations. The center focuses on conflicts in countries or regions that affect U.S. interests, but may be otherwise overlooked; where prevention appears possible; and when the resources of the Council on Foreign Relations can make a difference. The center does this by

- Issuing Council Special Reports to evaluate and respond rapidly to developing conflict situations and formulate timely, concrete policy recommendations that the U.S. government, international community, and local actors can use to limit the potential for deadly violence.
- Engaging the U.S. government and news media in conflict prevention efforts. CPA staff members meet with administration officials and members of Congress to brief on CPA's findings and recommendations; facilitate contacts between U.S. officials and important local and external actors; and raise awareness among journalists of potential flashpoints around the globe.
- Building networks with international organizations and institutions to complement and leverage the Council's established influence in the U.S. policy arena and increase the impact of CPA's recommendations.
- Providing a source of expertise on conflict prevention to include research, case studies, and lessons learned from past conflicts that policymakers and private citizens can use to prevent or mitigate future deadly conflicts.

# Council Special Reports

*Published by the Council on Foreign Relations*

*Partners in Preventive Action: The United States and International Institutions*
Paul B. Stares and Micah Zenko; CSR No. 62, September 2011
A Center for Preventive Action Report

*Justice Beyond The Hague: Supporting the Prosecution of International Crimes in National Courts*
David A. Kaye; CSR No. 61, June 2011

*The Drug War in Mexico: Confronting a Shared Threat*
David A. Shirk; CSR No. 60, March 2011
A Center for Preventive Action Report

*UN Security Council Enlargement and U.S. Interests*
Kara C. McDonald and Stewart M. Patrick; CSR No. 59, December 2010
An International Institutions and Global Governance Program Report

*Congress and National Security*
Kay King; CSR No. 58, November 2010

*Toward Deeper Reductions in U.S. and Russian Nuclear Weapons*
Micah Zenko; CSR No. 57, November 2010
A Center for Preventive Action Report

*Internet Governance in an Age of Cyber Insecurity*
Robert K. Knake; CSR No. 56, September 2010
An International Institutions and Global Governance Program Report

*From Rome to Kampala: The U.S. Approach to the 2010 International Criminal Court Review Conference*
Vijay Padmanabhan; CSR No. 55, April 2010

*Strengthening the Nuclear Nonproliferation Regime*
Paul Lettow; CSR No. 54, April 2010
An International Institutions and Global Governance Program Report

*The Russian Economic Crisis*
Jeffrey Mankoff; CSR No. 53, April 2010

*Somalia: A New Approach*
Bronwyn E. Bruton; CSR No. 52, March 2010
A Center for Preventive Action Report

*The Future of NATO*
James M. Goldgeier; CSR No. 51, February 2010
An International Institutions and Global Governance Program Report

*The United States in the New Asia*
Evan A. Feigenbaum and Robert A. Manning; CSR No. 50, November 2009
An International Institutions and Global Governance Program Report

*Intervention to Stop Genocide and Mass Atrocities: International Norms and U.S. Policy*
Matthew C. Waxman; CSR No. 49, October 2009
An International Institutions and Global Governance Program Report

*Enhancing U.S. Preventive Action*
Paul B. Stares and Micah Zenko; CSR No. 48, October 2009
A Center for Preventive Action Report

*The Canadian Oil Sands: Energy Security vs. Climate Change*
Michael A. Levi; CSR No. 47, May 2009
A Maurice R. Greenberg Center for Geoeconomic Studies Report

*The National Interest and the Law of the Sea*
Scott G. Borgerson; CSR No. 46, May 2009

*Lessons of the Financial Crisis*
Benn Steil; CSR No. 45, March 2009
A Maurice R. Greenberg Center for Geoeconomic Studies Report

*Global Imbalances and the Financial Crisis*
Steven Dunaway; CSR No. 44, March 2009
A Maurice R. Greenberg Center for Geoeconomic Studies Report

*Eurasian Energy Security*
Jeffrey Mankoff; CSR No. 43, February 2009

*Preparing for Sudden Change in North Korea*
Paul B. Stares and Joel S. Wit; CSR No. 42, January 2009
A Center for Preventive Action Report

*Averting Crisis in Ukraine*
Steven Pifer; CSR No. 41, January 2009
A Center for Preventive Action Report

*Congo: Securing Peace, Sustaining Progress*
Anthony W. Gambino; CSR No. 40, October 2008
A Center for Preventive Action Report

*Deterring State Sponsorship of Nuclear Terrorism*
Michael A. Levi; CSR No. 39, September 2008

*China, Space Weapons, and U.S. Security*
Bruce W. MacDonald; CSR No. 38, September 2008

*Sovereign Wealth and Sovereign Power: The Strategic Consequences of American Indebtedness*
Brad W. Setser; CSR No. 37, September 2008
A Maurice R. Greenberg Center for Geoeconomic Studies Report

*Securing Pakistan's Tribal Belt*
Daniel Markey; CSR No. 36, July 2008 (Web-only release) and August 2008
A Center for Preventive Action Report

*Avoiding Transfers to Torture*
Ashley S. Deeks; CSR No. 35, June 2008

*Global FDI Policy: Correcting a Protectionist Drift*
David M. Marchick and Matthew J. Slaughter; CSR No. 34, June 2008
A Maurice R. Greenberg Center for Geoeconomic Studies Report

*Dealing with Damascus: Seeking a Greater Return on U.S.-Syria Relations*
Mona Yacoubian and Scott Lasensky; CSR No. 33, June 2008
A Center for Preventive Action Report

*Climate Change and National Security: An Agenda for Action*
Joshua W. Busby; CSR No. 32, November 2007
A Maurice R. Greenberg Center for Geoeconomic Studies Report

*Planning for Post-Mugabe Zimbabwe*
Michelle D. Gavin; CSR No. 31, October 2007
A Center for Preventive Action Report

*The Case for Wage Insurance*
Robert J. LaLonde; CSR No. 30, September 2007
A Maurice R. Greenberg Center for Geoeconomic Studies Report

*Reform of the International Monetary Fund*
Peter B. Kenen; CSR No. 29, May 2007
A Maurice R. Greenberg Center for Geoeconomic Studies Report

*Nuclear Energy: Balancing Benefits and Risks*
Charles D. Ferguson; CSR No. 28, April 2007

*Nigeria: Elections and Continuing Challenges*
Robert I. Rotberg; CSR No. 27, April 2007
A Center for Preventive Action Report

*The Economic Logic of Illegal Immigration*
Gordon H. Hanson; CSR No. 26, April 2007
A Maurice R. Greenberg Center for Geoeconomic Studies Report

*The United States and the WTO Dispute Settlement System*
Robert Z. Lawrence; CSR No. 25, March 2007
A Maurice R. Greenberg Center for Geoeconomic Studies Report

*Bolivia on the Brink*
Eduardo A. Gamarra; CSR No. 24, February 2007
A Center for Preventive Action Report

*After the Surge: The Case for U.S. Military Disengagement from Iraq*
Steven N. Simon; CSR No. 23, February 2007

*Darfur and Beyond: What Is Needed to Prevent Mass Atrocities*
Lee Feinstein; CSR No. 22, January 2007

*Avoiding Conflict in the Horn of Africa: U.S. Policy Toward Ethiopia and Eritrea*
Terrence Lyons; CSR No. 21, December 2006
A Center for Preventive Action Report

*Living with Hugo: U.S. Policy Toward Hugo Chávez's Venezuela*
Richard Lapper; CSR No. 20, November 2006
A Center for Preventive Action Report

*Reforming U.S. Patent Policy: Getting the Incentives Right*
Keith E. Maskus; CSR No. 19, November 2006
A Maurice R. Greenberg Center for Geoeconomic Studies Report

*Foreign Investment and National Security: Getting the Balance Right*
Alan P. Larson and David M. Marchick; CSR No. 18, July 2006
A Maurice R. Greenberg Center for Geoeconomic Studies Report

*Challenges for a Postelection Mexico: Issues for U.S. Policy*
Pamela K. Starr; CSR No. 17, June 2006 (Web-only release) and November 2006

*U.S.-India Nuclear Cooperation: A Strategy for Moving Forward*
Michael A. Levi and Charles D. Ferguson; CSR No. 16, June 2006

*Generating Momentum for a New Era in U.S.-Turkey Relations*
Steven A. Cook and Elizabeth Sherwood-Randall; CSR No. 15, June 2006

*Peace in Papua: Widening a Window of Opportunity*
Blair A. King; CSR No. 14, March 2006
A Center for Preventive Action Report

*Neglected Defense: Mobilizing the Private Sector to Support Homeland Security*
Stephen E. Flynn and Daniel B. Prieto; CSR No. 13, March 2006

*Afghanistan's Uncertain Transition From Turmoil to Normalcy*
Barnett R. Rubin; CSR No. 12, March 2006
A Center for Preventive Action Report

*Preventing Catastrophic Nuclear Terrorism*
Charles D. Ferguson; CSR No. 11, March 2006

*Getting Serious About the Twin Deficits*
Menzie D. Chinn; CSR No. 10, September 2005
A Maurice R. Greenberg Center for Geoeconomic Studies Report

*Both Sides of the Aisle: A Call for Bipartisan Foreign Policy*
Nancy E. Roman; CSR No. 9, September 2005

*Forgotten Intervention? What the United States Needs to Do in the Western Balkans*
Amelia Branczik and William L. Nash; CSR No. 8, June 2005
A Center for Preventive Action Report

*A New Beginning: Strategies for a More Fruitful Dialogue with the Muslim World*
Craig Charney and Nicole Yakatan; CSR No. 7, May 2005

*Power-Sharing in Iraq*
David L. Phillips; CSR No. 6, April 2005
A Center for Preventive Action Report

*Giving Meaning to "Never Again": Seeking an Effective Response to the Crisis in Darfur and Beyond*
Cheryl O. Igiri and Princeton N. Lyman; CSR No. 5, September 2004

*Freedom, Prosperity, and Security: The G8 Partnership with Africa: Sea Island 2004 and Beyond*
J. Brian Atwood, Robert S. Browne, and Princeton N. Lyman; CSR No. 4, May 2004

*Addressing the HIV/AIDS Pandemic: A U.S. Global AIDS Strategy for the Long Term*
Daniel M. Fox and Princeton N. Lyman; CSR No. 3, May 2004
Cosponsored with the Milbank Memorial Fund

*Challenges for a Post-Election Philippines*
Catharin E. Dalpino; CSR No. 2, May 2004
A Center for Preventive Action Report

*Stability, Security, and Sovereignty in the Republic of Georgia*
David L. Phillips; CSR No. 1, January 2004
A Center for Preventive Action Report

To purchase a printed copy, call the Brookings Institution Press: 800.537.5487.
*Note:* Council Special Reports are available for download from CFR's website, www.cfr.org.
For more information, email publications@cfr.org.